T0304398

FISH CARCASS

VICTUALS, SPASMS, CORPORALITY

ALSO BY VI KHI NAO

SWIMMING WITH DEAD STARS
THE VEGAS DILEMMA
A BELL CURVE IS A PREGNANT STRAIGHT LINE
HUMAN TETRIS
SHEEP MACHINE
UMBILICAL HOSPITAL
A BRIEF ALPHABET OF TORTURE
FISH IN EXILE
THE OLD PHILOSOPHER

FISH

VI KHI NAO

CARCASS

BLACK SUN LIT

BROOKLYN / ARKVILLE, NY
2022

Black Sun Lit
c/o Jared D. Fagen
PO Box 307
Arkville, NY 11406
www.blacksunlit.com | @BlackSunLit

Printed in the United States of America by Bookmobile
www.bookmobile.com

Distributed by Small Press Distribution
www.spdbooks.org

Black Sun Lit publications and programs are made possible by the New York State Council on the Arts with the support of the Office of the Governor and the New York State Legislature.

Artwork: Vi Khi Nao

CONTENTS

CORPORALITY

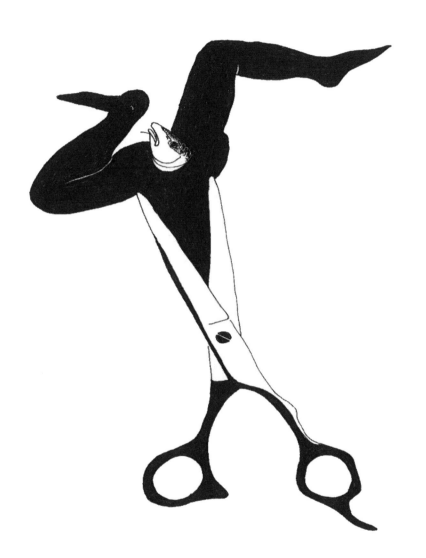

VICTUALS

THE BINCHŌTAN CHARCOAL & ITS ASH

There is no delusion that she wants her.
Is marriage like owning a very expensive art piece?

Your spouse the painting?
You the crooked frame that won't fit?

Is this how desire is born?
From having less or from wanting more?

She wakes up calling her name.
She wakes up knowing that she doesn't want less.

From *House of Cards* she learned a new rule: "I love that
woman. I love her more than sharks love blood."

Or something along those lines. She may have misquoted.
It came out of the pre-disgraced Kevin Spacey's mouth.

Her God doesn't exercise telepathy or residence.
Hands, eyes, mouths, authenticity.
It's a city without mirrors.
Because touch, in itself, is symmetry.

*

She held the woman's face in her mind's eye &
realized that they would never be lovers &
as soon as she let her go, moss grew all over
the geography of her hands and the woman's face.

Is this because it's a debt that must be paid for
not believing in somebody.
In herself?

She felt the desire of desire as if it were a binchōtan
charcoal and its ash.

Masakichi Yakitori
and the Pyramid Club.

*

On Easter Sunday, she sang a Lao Tzu Christmas carol.
Lao Tzu, where is your power to persuade a tree from
falling asleep on itself?

Does night dream of actresses sleeping on leaves?
Where is the human figure in this?

Your Saturday is a memory without a body.
A pair of lungs that knew too much about your mother's
rape tell you to leave reality through the threshold of a
dream.

You knew how to be authentic. How to get rid of people.
How desertion works in the wilderness.
You exclude sound from your thesis.
It's a way for you to desert poetry without being too poetic.

*

There were thistles inside of your mother's vaginal canal.

She wasn't violated in the wilderness. He has dragged her
there to say that it is okay to want pins and needles. She
wasn't numbed after all. Her body didn't pretend to be a
God. Just a whimpered Lao Tzu.

In a remote mountain, the men are smoking pipes and their
vapors smell like evergreen.

To punctuate their desire she says: God is being difficult.
But he is not.

I have to tell the world that I am sad and have been
forgotten. Is there a way home from not being homeless? Is
there a way to swim in an Indian Reservation without being
caught?

Listen: the isotope was just a trope.
There are ways to move smoothly in and out of insincerity.

We grow to learn how to brush melted butter
onto dough shaped like the cavalry.
They arrive galloping on baking
sheets without yeast in their armors.

*

Every Tuesday we acquire clues from the shape
of your mother's scream.
When it was hoarse, it had the shape of a small bonsai tree.

Your cat licks you and licks you.

You know it's not 300 B.C.
Desire comes and goes while leaving lies to clothe
itself.

Her anger is a troublesome candidate of sadness—
lights itself on fire.
From time to time, the cunt of that fire grows ember by
ember.

Once in a while, a house made of screams floats down a
black river on the planet Pluto.
Its chimney is not designed to ventilate silence or
resilience.
It's designed to allow screams to escape without
suffocating everyone inside.

Once in a while the rain arrives to suppress the anger of the
scream.

When anger soaks like wet grasses on the house's
floorboard, the ants come out to showcase their military
might.

They resurrect the screams from their wet ash and carry
them on their powerful backs.
The aftermath of a rape is portable and transmutable.
A possible somatic experience for the ants, but may not be
for the human or the inhuman.

TARRAGON, ARE YOU A WILD BOAR?

Tarragon, are you a wild boar?
My friend, lemon zest, has not been that
Thyme, Cognac, *falooda* glass noodle
These things prowl the night without cape
Gooseberries or bacalao

Tarragon, are you a wild boar?
Each time I eat you, I stop breathing
Little owl, where is your happiness?
Wake up + make people believe
In you, gastrique + steaklette
Is that chive embarrassed?
To be with the savoy cabbage?

Tarragon, are you a wild boar?
I was born female, hyper-focused
Let me trim your skirt, halibut
It's dragging salt against my oregano
Buttered by butter in no butter

Tarragon, are you a wild boar?
It's too bad the caper isn't wearing
A cape when the Peruvian potatoes
Are sitting on a bed of coals while
Floating down a river coconut
On the verge of falling off
A truffle, which is a
Shadow floating inside of a shadow

FISH CARCASS

fish carcass
say hello to pork rind
+ arborio rice
while castaway caraway puree returns
home to deconstruct wilted carrot
from its butter + herb remnants

fish carcass
say goodbye to a knife fight
between under-marinated onion slice
+ wasted redbor kale
amidst a gun battle between
grilled salmon + paprika

fish carcass
say goodnight to electrolytes + magnesium
as a chemical imbalance takes
place inside the borderline cod meat

fish carcass
say good morning to anti-griddle + orange liqueur
whose pre-conditional love for salt + bitterness
reminiscent of caviar + pancetta vinaigrette
has put quail eggs
under the cloche

fish carcass
say midday to emu eggs while
the sun twirls
inside a decadent basket of

fish sauce without making
the plastic mattress, walk-in
refrigerator, + bacon sabayon
feel left out

fish carcass
say cloud nine
say egginess
say shell-shocked
say cornichon
say it angelo
say italian meringue
say calf liver
say republic of georgia
say lavash
say turnpipe turnips
say succotash
say yuzu marmalade
say overcooked quail
say chef teah evans
say fish head
say into a barrel
say bacon fat
say baby corn
say flavor profile
say with victory
say the gods are with me
say no guts no glory
say did not materialize
say story on a plate

THERE IS NO TOUCHDOWN HERE, BELICHICK

I love it when the head coaches of the NFL cover their
mouths when they verbalize their game plans
I wonder if the ocean ever covers its lips whenever
the river opens wide its mouth to disclose its plan to
drown all the carps and catfish through plastic poisoning
I expect the carps to put on their football helmets to defend
    its life from plastic
I expect the quarterbacks in the form of
phytoplankon to lead the rivers out of hell
When it is January again and the Superbowl hasn't fallen
    asleep on my lap
I take the salmon to bed with me
and press a warm hand on its cold body
While it dies slowly in my arms
I know a fresh wild fish never makes a good face mask
I know I can't resolve my daddy issues by whispering all my
    secrets to a dead fish
I know that even when I don't cover my face
my life strategy can be read by everyone
Including those who are not even my opponents
Because my secret is that all along
I just want to die with that grill-bearing craniate
In that bed of mine that no one would dare to say is
    anybody's riverbed

SALIVA TERRACADE

Your tongue is lightweight
Like ceramic tiles
While you lick
Your lover in order to
Build a saliva-based
Terracade
You may be Shane
Henrik, Australian,
Architect, building
Your cubistic blocks
But Picasso beats
You to it without
Resorting to enzyme
Lubrication, bacterial
Decay or mucosal
Refusal, and the
Submandibular Gland is
Simply a glance away

SEISMIC SEA WAVE

It's not incidental
But is it possible
For lettuce to be
Spanked by whale
Oil? Or turned
Nordic in the Winter
Months if salted
Herring takes
Dance classes with Redzepi?

Kissing is not molecular
Neither is lipstick or
Raspberry reduction
It's about making whale's blood
An exterior like lipstick + waiting for chefs
To give birth to frozen strawberries
On a table where walruses get walloped
By doctors as they return home
With tsunamis in their bellies

COITAL EXPOSURE

Women who don't date men
Compensate for their lack of
Coital exposure by
Imbibing basil seed drink
+ eating spring rolls
Whose translucent skins
Divulge bulgy juicy veins
+ greens: cucumber, green onion,
Shrimp, pork, barbequed beef
Basil, cilantro, avocado
Revealing the verdant penis
As something that dips
Well with peanut sauce
But technically so much
Better with nước mắm
The female organ as
Squid in liquid form.

CLUSTERS OF SILHOUETTES

If you look into
The star inside
My body

Clusters of
Silhouettes

Flask of light

You know

Bundles of dark light
I carry across the room
The fish concealed
Between your legs

To measure
The anxiety
Of desiring
You mid-morning
To late
After

Noon

Swimming
Is only a page
Of turning
You over

See

The stove
Which the skillet
Asks the hand
To remove its only
Tongue

You swim
Inside
(Beneath
The quiet drawer)
Me

Quickly
As if tongue
Is born
To catch

You
Swinging
Between two
Crying lyres

STALK OF PIADINA

Bread + blood inside mesclum
Suppressing babyfish from a
Diabolic diavolo

Stalk of rosemary
Can you fake fear?

Stalk of piadina
What about you?

Diabolic diavolo
Can you fake fear?

Death lies on the table
Giving baths to ineloquence

BLOOD PAPAYA

Let's have a compote duel:
Sweet against sweet
Liqueur against liqueur

Conceptually, I love you
Earthy truffle oil
The pressure to be with you
Is raw garlic
May require
A summer to
Wake up in
The pantry
With you

Blow it, game birds
While I move my
Ass to cherry bing
Sodium low
Lower than martini
Lower than sodium agnolotti

VEAL TONGUE

I feel transported already
During this brief flight
Out of veal tongue
The spotlight is obviously
On the visual impact
The mung bean is strapped
On the back of a roasted
Suckling pig
Which is also riding on my
Tongue

MOLECULAR SOUP

Thinks about
Wave-riding techniques
In a ceramic bowl

If the tongue is
A snowboard
What is Snow?

BERNARD LOISEAU IS DEAD

Bernard Loiseau is dead
Pistol
Penetrating
Sour cream
And beetroot
Frozen dots of reality
On a sirloin plate
This is death not
Being so sirloin

GODDESS OF WAR

sapphire
goddess of war
bishamon in liver sauce
      in guinea fowl salad
      in fettuccina
      in eel
faith beyond the dish
necessary for credibility

GOD IS IGNEOUS

God is igneous
God is sedimentary
God is metamorphic
        is made of heat
+ pressure
+ forced to cool down
To lie still
Like a Barbie doll in a Coma
While stone plays
Hide + seek with strata
A corporeal visibility
Almost as if God
Lives inside
A graduation
Of colossal proportions

LICKING LIGHT

Light unlocks her sins
Licking dark light like a lizard's tongue

The afternoon breaks open
Her music of radiance

The door is rolling on
The floor

And the colors of yesterday
Sunbathe in the shade

After all, the antithesis of desire
Is hair growing backward into the knees

And men crawling back into their graves
Children mowing the lawn without heads

Mothers folding their arms in wooden crates
Grandmothers giving hickeys to bruised plums

TRANSCRIPTS AFTER EMPTINESS: ON INCUBATION AND RAPTURE [i]

This sparkle, after the great forfeiture, fathered vacuity. Her
    mounting nerves at a loss.

After the fright, seizure in prolonged tenderness.

Our desires—she clamps in her private closet for me.

Below the orchard: an unwieldy climate, burdened
with crystal. Extra-large to counter the atmosphere of
dampness—a lover's heart, feasibly—never comfortable
about releasing fear.

Her offspring unbuttons fragrances of verdant madness,
    hung to the tributary by a cedar tree.

If a sapling has to die, why not for bereaved moonlight? Its
    happiness, muted by light.

Abandoned in a rental car, love would fade, jokingly; not
    really.

* * *

It's possible to surrender now, after the body resists rapture

But a blouse forgives—

---

[i] Mia Ayumi Malhotra, "Notes from the Birth Year: On Gestation and
Becoming"

While waiting for spring to arrive—her ears close their
doors, patiently delaying the echoes from departing the
room—as

A river, not yet employed by the Milky Way, steps into the
body of another river—

To change the discourse of time

But hunger, doubt, emptiness—these all travel flippantly,
casually without lovers

Stabbing their backs

* * *

The summers came and departed, leaving verdant holes in
the sweaters of winter

Kiss me in the afternoon and I will tell you everything

Not shattered nor shamed by flight of resistance

Our enemies dressed in rice noodles delivered on a moped

To incubate is not easy, it's easier to watch the eggs cross the
street than the chickens

Every step counts, despite what the statistics of hit & run
tell us

Don't be deceived by the fake changes we see & report

We all throw our children into the garbage bins because we know they have a high tolerance for insomnia

So stab the night if you want; it won't get you very far

SPASMS

SLEEP

Clocking in
159 hours of
overtime
in a month
averaging
5.3 hours of
excess work
each day on
8 hours worth
of daily labor
The laborer
Miwa Sado
is placing her
small nippon
head on the
train track
of Japanese
work culture
waiting for
the sleeper of
karōshi
to escort
her heart
failure to
Tokyo
where labor
laws have fallen
asleep
Not forced
at all to clock in

159 hours
of overtime
to slaughter
overtime
Not forced
to endure years
of chronic sleep
deprivation
Not forced
to jump out
of a building
Silence is diligent
Exhaustion is diligent
Death is diligent
Suicide is diligent
Not sleeping is diligent
What is the opposite
of diligence?
An eager
tongue that
would devastate
the following
demographic:
Slothful
raw tuna
taking a nap on
a bed of sushi rice
on a Friday afternoon
Sluggish
eels
taking forty winks
with wasabi & its

indolent workmate
soy sauce
Inactive
calamari
vegging out with
its unrelated
lethargic relatives:
Cucumbers
& avocados
Premium Friday is
not Medium Monday
Premium is not
Premium
The last Friday of
the month for
unrequired leisure
is the equivalent
of asking
if two extra
rice seeds
would nourish
the human
body for
a year

ABYSS

Walking her
Walking her
Walking her
Naked
They are walking her
To the outer edge
Where water meets delirium
Where they toss her
Into the boat
They toss another naked man
In
With her
Before tossing him
They tell him,
You may rape her now, Brother
Of course he rapes her
But before then
In the dark
They roll
Roll the boat in sand
Where the two
Plunge sideways
Tossing like rolls of dice
His penis bounces against
Her body
Like a stick against a drum
Before he rapes her
Before they nail the lid
Of the boat like a coffin
They nail and nail and nail

They flip the boat
So the hull is pressed, dug into sand
They keep on
Pounding away
Pounding
She fears the nails
May rape her
Impale her
To the edge
Of their dreams
To the edge
Of their violence
To the edge
Of his sunset
Where she suffocates
Where he suffocates
While still inside her
When the darkness
Transfixes her silhouette
To a star
Stamped at the bottom
Of her butt hole
Her blood is a silhouette
A star
Stillborn
Their violence
Is a hut lit on fire
To delineate
To define
Her mouth
Which is
The center
Of her volition

CAVITY

You defecate
Then you get raped
Or you get raped
Then you can
Defecate
To defeat rape
All women in
India should stop
Eating
Samosa, biryani, chicken tikka masala, tandoori lamb, roti,
panipuri, chapatti, jalebi, dosa, palak paneer, naan, chana
masala, keema, papadum, pav bhaji, raita, korma, pakora,
vindaloo, shahi paneer, laddu, dal makhani, kheer, idli,
dhokla, rasgulla, ras malai, sambar, aloo gobi, khichdi, chole
bhature, vada pav, sheer khuma, rogan josh, hyderabadi
biryani, modak, vada, kulfi, sabudana khichdi
Frequently,
Habitually,
Routinely,
Repeatedly,
Regularly,
Recurrently,
Continually,
And, specifically as in customarily
Meanwhile
Men in India
Could continue to eat
And continue to defecate
Naturally
Fearlessly

To avoid waste
Of toilet paper
They should use
Women's toes
Faces hands sleeves breasts hair
To wash away
Feces
Still clung
Tight to their
Male emporium

ENNUI

I had to sodomize
My British education
With fascism
& trade in
My ophthalmic
Proficiency & expertise
For a civil war bathed
In malice, demolition,
Destruction &
Chemical rivalry
My wife is a rose
My children are
Aristocratically sheltered
& pre-dictatorial
Not exposed to
Sarin, the toxic gas
I had released
Into the Idlib air
To combat
Historical anomaly
Five millions of
My people had
Fled outside of my
Sphere of affluence
I guess they couldn't
Wait to find out if
I would excel in
Multitasking:
Being an eye doctor
To my country & also

Being popular in the field
Of totalitarianism
I am told I am
Exquisite on the
Operating table
I have the ability
To make people
See what I could not
See: the power of
My surgical precision
The nepotic offspring of
My father's vision
Against Israel
And, now that I have
Fallen in love with Russia
Just as a precaution
Instead of closing both eyes,
Should I keep half an eye
Open & half an eye
Closed while I operate
On my grandmother's
Uveal coloboma?

DESPAIR

Boko

VOID

I am not sure if this is
A Libyan move
But with 3K dead at sea
East of Tripoli
I cling to my mother's lifeless body
She is my lifeboat
My elevator
Up from liquid purgatory
Our rubber dinghy
Deflated, lopsided
Not designed for
153 Guineans, Malians,
Senegalans, Cameroonians, etc.
The Italians
Are busy being Rome
But not Romans
I am three years old
My youth is my asylum
And, my asylum is
My aunt
Sub-Saharan Africa
Is really beautiful
Despite the persecution
The wars that are too big
For my body
Am I an economic migrant?
Afterwards,
After I am forced
To repatriate
Would you abduct me

If you were a Libyan
Coastguard?
Resell me
Back to my uncle?
My cousin
Bound in history by
Exilic and cruel
Yahya Jammeh?
Would my country
Confuse me
For a three year old
Diabolical
HIV medical care
Scheme?
Soften your blow
I am not as
Boring
Or repetitive
Or insipid
As you may be lead
To believe
We are only
1 Billion dollars
In debt
For most Italians
I am a burden
And my childhood
Waits for no one
For extradition
My flight is no
Leisured Saturday
Someday,

If I am lucky,
I will sit next to
An infomercial

UNITED

Cara Delevingne
Gwyneth Paltrow
Angelina Jolie
Alice Evans
Amber Anderson
Ambra Battilana Gutierrez
Angie Everhart
Ashley Judd
Asia Argento
Claire Forlani
Dawn Dunning
Emily Nestor
Emma de Caunes
Florence Darel
Gymnasts
Jessica Barth
Judith Godreche
Heather Graham
Kate Beckinsale
Katherine Kendall
Katya Mtsitouridze
Laura Madden
Lauren Sivan
Lauren O'Connor
Lea Seydoux
Lena Headey
Liza Campell
Louisette Geiss
Louise Godbold
Lucia Evans

Lupita Nyong'o
Lysette Anthony
Marisa Goughlan
Melissa Sagemiller
Mia Kirshner
Mimi Haleyi
Minka Kelly
Mira Sorvino
Romola Garai
Rose McGowan
Rosanna Arquette
Sarah Ann Masse
Sarah Smith
Sophie Dix
Tara Subkoff
Tomi-Ann Roberts
Trish Goff
Unnamed Women
Vu Thu Phuong
Zelda Perkins
Zoe Brock

STATES

Al Franken
Andrew Kreisberg
Andy Dick
Andy Signore
Ben Affleck
Ben Baker
Benjamin Genocchio
Brett Ratner
Charlie Rose
Chris Savino
David Guillod
Dustin Hoffman
Donald Trump
Ed Westwick
Eddie Berganza
George H.W. Bush
Glenn Thrush
Hamilton Fish
Harvey Weinstein
James Toback
Jeff Hoover
Jeffrey Tambor
Jeremy Piven
John Lasseter
Josh Besh
Kevin Spacey
Kirt Webster
Knight Landesman
Larry Nassar
Leon Wieseltier

Lockhart Steele
Louis C.K.
Mark Halperin
Matt Lauer
Matt Zimmerman
Michael Oreskes
Oliver Stone
Rick Najera
Robert Scoble
Roy Moore
Roy Price
Steve Wynn
Steve Jurvetson
Steven Seagal
Terry Richardson

CORPORALITY

MY EXISTENCE

suicide attempt #1
suicide attempt #2
suicide attempt #3
suicide attempt #4
suicide attempt #5
suicide attempt #6
suicide attempt #7
suicide attempt #8
suicide attempt #9
suicide attempt #10
suicide attempt #11
suicide attempt #12
suicide attempt #13
suicide attempt #14
suicdie attempt #15
suicide attempt #16
suicide attempt #17
suicide attempt #18
suicide attempt #19
suicide attempt #20
suicide attempt #21
suicide attempt #22
suicide attempt #23
suicide attempt #24
suicide attempt #25
suicide attempt #26
suicide attempt #27
suicide attempt #28
suicide attempt #28
suicide attempt #30
suicide attempt #32

MY MOUTH

To clothe my mouth
I kiss you

To clothe my desire
I make love to you

To clothe my soul
I disappear into you

To clothe my eyes
I grow perennial flowers

To clothe my bones
I drink milk

To clothe the night
I become unfriendly with light

To clothe time
I talk to God

To clothe rain
I embrace the adverbial clouds

To clothe my heart
I start a savings account

To clothe my ears
I fall in love with Orpheus

MY FACE

When he rode me on his motorcycle,
The wind shook my face like a glass of water
When I climbed down from the bike
My face spilled all over me

MY SPINE

Sadness tore me from light
Under a brick tree
A tree dressed in cement and brick
Where earth becomes firewood
And soot, leaves
Ghastly ghosts of photosynthesis
Travel up and down
My spine
Where bones become
Segments of time
And sky
The ultimate symbol
Of suffocation

MY EARS

Tomorrow I will ask a book to hug a tree
And a tree to hug its own branch
Then I will ask my mother to hug me
Because today I have already hugged myself
Between procrastination and self-love
I choose to invert
The eco-friendly on myself.
Someday I will cut down a tree
And ask Israel to go to war with Hamas
And unask myself to unhug
The corridor between me
And the world
From within
The largest outdoor prison system
Is screaming at
My eardrums like fireflies

MY SPLEEN

Infinity drifts out of your soul
Like snow while
You are sitting in front of a fire
Trying to blow out the
Wind in your chest

A small fire which leaves
Tears running out of my body
Rain runs after pavement, you say

The meters of the night
Drill holes into
My spleen, says the earth

What if love is not
The petrified wood
of yesterday?

Would you marry the day
With the night?

MY FEET

I ask God to bind
Me to you
The way the Chinese
Bound the feet of
Their women
So when you see me
Walking with you
We are two
Tortured flasks
Waving goodbye
To one another

MY ARMS

Words are sleepwalking
Around my mind
I tell them to go to sleep
So I can go to sleep
I pull words by the sleeves
Beg them to come to bed with me
They refuse to
Continue to somnambulate
Not like an ambulance
In a hurry to get to the hospital
After the gunman wounded
Nearly 500 folks and killed 58 people
No, they walk like
Jaywalkers, not heeding stop signs
Made by the signals
Of my frustrations
I gather the words into my arms
Ask each one to fall asleep
Like senescent babies
I would croak them into telling me
Their relationship to insomnia
Which they don't know exists
What kind of synthetic vitamins
Will they take?
Before they lose their bodies
To my memory?

MY TONGUE

In the dark
my heart echoes
its own door
Each echo
a sound born to
deceive the eyes
that could not listen
to the movement below
my button hole

You are my immortal beloved
Why don't you stretch
your eyes out + let me
blink between the sheets
with my tongue
I roll below the snow

You are the cow that
hasn't been made to milk
my resignation day in
and day out

I'd love to drop the astral belt on
your thighs + call it divisions
of being buried alive

You + I are made for the
guttural rebound

After our love is dead

will you bury me alive?
with your 2,000 wives?

What is this tomorrow
but the will
to say goodbye?

MY MEMORY

You have fallen into my memory
Like rain
And I, wishing to deplete you,
Open my umbrella
Are there times when
We aren't children or lovers?
Even thunderstorms breathe in electricity
Where grasses
Deteriorate under the moonlight
Are we enemies or lightning rods?
Are we substance or are we merely gods?
I am amber and you are light
Let's swallow each other until
We are swollen
Tumescent moons wiggling
Inside the throat of twilight

MY HEART

The rose isn't afraid to
Die having dyed its
Hair purple, the color
Of death.

Several ozone layers later,
The rose isn't afraid to
Give birth to a firing
Squad of leaves, stems
Drawing amphoral bullets
From the roots spreading
Deep + wide.

Below the waist of time,
Sedimentary pose for
Cemented soil + volcanic
Ruptures.

The rose, after emitting a
Pollution of love, is now
Ready to conquer daylight
Seeing time, where darkness
Has woken up less darkness
From its nocturnal core.

With my heart dipped in ice,
"Now I wake up from a
dream," says the rose.

MY STOMACH

My stomach is a baby
Duckling waddling
In red paint, in isolation, in solitude
And, from time to time
I would look over this waterbird
This solitary confinement
With my shoulders and shrug
My red paint into a green room
There are arms pulling, pulling
Me into the sea
But, when you placed my night into a Ziplock bag
Its invisible plastic zipper
Clearly not working
And, leaking out - the fog, the snow, the
Ineloquent misdirection of your full, buried kiss
Which has never been a good mother to me
Because a good mother
Knows how to abandon
My breath, at the right time
At the right place, a place
Where a waterbird, hydrating in an abortion,
could not breathe

MY SKIN

Because I dream of you as skin and door…
I know you have been sublime before
As engorged
As distorted as my view of the world

If I could surrender your name
Your lips
Your invasion
Toward more heroic hours
I would be asking you to sling
Your kiss forward as if to
Kill what isn't saliva, which isn't the fiberglass of the tongue
before losing its small war to frozen elasticity, which is what
our bodies could do before language knew how to sin

& now whenever I fuck you, you are subdued
Some call it weed
But I call it a vegetable garden that invites ant extermination
    and cabbage fascism
Alas, your front door lies open and your eyes a drop or two
    of virgin olive oil
In which I pour your gaze over a skillet
It swims next to a small yellow lake called clitoris
& do take note
This isn't ardor but death on an open stove

Which is what fucking is…
Before breakfast before the tongue
Retrieves its own clamor from the wind

You were my kind before I was your kind
When we intertwine, your bones cleave
To my skin like knives being
Pulled out a chiffon cake

I bruise hard before I bruise slow
And although I am no engine of light
My blight is that I was never yours
And you were never mine
Says a beehive to its despotic queen

MY BODY

When the bus drives home the
   sun is swimming behind
     the trees

I missed the bus while trying
   to text

Even the earth knows
   it can't clothe itself
   in pure ecstasy

Even yesterday Autumn forgets
   her own childbirth

My entire body is made
   out of sin

Even God knows it's hard to
   give birth to
   baby manic depression

It's hard to distinguish
   what lives behind you
   + what lives inside you

Yesterday the trees have
   been tortured
   by a gang of wet clouds

And the snowbank dreams
   of flattening the mosquitos

MY SOUL

I can't feel the bullet
Made entirely from
The evening gown
Of ennui lodged
In my soul
Just as you can't feel
The fiberglass of
My desire dressed
Like God's mistress
Reframing the coeval
Landscape of my sex
My time on earth
Has a soul just as your
Time in me, made
From the pipeline
Of infinity, is soulless
Earth, you are my inmate
Time, you are my wife
God, you are my rebirth
Sky, you are my daughter
While my daughter
Sweeps the cloud floor
With her broom, the tornado,
And while my inmate is too
Busy making love to my wife
Won't you tell your
Discrete mass of
Gray matter or your
Particle of quantum
Light to give me

Radiation so I
Can exist outside
Of this electromagnetic
Accident called life?

MY YEAR

The year I was supposed to die, I don't die
I see my body before her eyes
Our reticent voice of intimacy
When it was awkward and lovely between us
As my attempt to slow down
The passion that is slowly brewing between us
Like smothered coffee in a trash bag

I don't care what happens
I just want to die right away
Then I remember
I can't
My mother has at least ten years to live
And suicide must be a lover I must learn to discard at any
    moment's notice
I wonder what my lover thinks of me
The way I treat her like suicide, stringing her along
I want to have you, but not yet
Tomorrow my mother is eating kale
And is very healthy & doesn't smoke or drink & does yoga
and has the strength & energy and vitality of a 20 year old
boy

MY FREEZING SOLAR

How long have you been sleeping, Snow?
In that white sparking consciousness of yours
If your sleep is champagne
Mine is whiskey on ice
Shadow buries its tongue on shadow
Our lives are burning backward + forward
Obtuse tongue says, Hello Everybody.
I am a weaker form of deformity, says one dying snowflake
As it descends the stairless octave of earth
I have given birth to a dismal landscape
My army of sleeping men
Swollen by Carpathian crystalline
Your cloud my granular
My hail your pellets of warmth
Your lake my evaporation
Your smell extratropical
My windward your equivalent
You sublimate
You castigate
Your downslope love
My freezing solar
And it's Spring again
Layer by layer
While you glaciate
+ while I slowly move backward into your mouth

MY GLAMOROUS BOX

In Vegas, I live in a box. In a beautiful box for 4.5 months. And, it looks like this:

Where the light is miraculous.
There are radiations in my winter. My summer is skydiving.

I have been waking up in a cloud of fog. This weightlessness that is filled with liquid deterrent.

Each morning I wake up I hear the faint echo of a piano, of someone playing a piano, from the far receding center of the light. I am in Sin City and I shouldn't expect to hear the faint sound of a piano like sonic water droplets, but I do.

Should you practice what you preach?
Not necessarily.
There is virtue in hypocrisy. It's hard to find virtues, but I am making progress.

Ah. Lovely. Elton John has a private jet. And, he was very close to Princess Diana. Who wouldn't be? Except Harry's father. For environmental reasons, the Duke and Duchess made four trips in 11 days. One of those trips, courtesy of Elton John and husband, David, was for Harry and Meghan to come and visit them in their mansion in Nice to celebrate Meghan's birthday.

Is there carbon equity if one owns a private aircraft and is not able to use it?
Are we able to label something as accumulating carbon foot-print if we let (extraordinary) resources such as a private jet accumulate dust?

An   exploding   star   places   its   cellphone
In   his   pocket
And says the following—
"I don't want to pee out any more intergalactic/
diuretic cosmic dust. I want my body to belong to my
own   cosmos.   But   Wunderland—"

Its   phone   blooms   out   a   tulip   in   reply
And buries its heart in a flowerpot.

Surface dictator
Surface dictator
Surface dictator

"I wish you could see the radiation beneath your eyelids."

Meanwhile there is a piano at Elton John's Nice villa.

Below	the	surface	of	itself
Until		my		dictator
And		my		dictation
My amanuensis starts to retaliate against my formlessness				

Dr. Potassium
Dr. Potassium
Should I take you home with me? To cure my diuretic.
An exploding star is worried, "What if, what if, I pee out all of my minerals?"
Meanwhile I am lacking in electrolytes. I get dizzy when I stand up. I am seeing stars. My heart muscles are getting weak. My blood pressure is too low. Could someone smell the immigrational status of a dying star? And, it's not true that the antidote to pain is connection. The antidote to pain is to have a piano near a riverbed. The river runs its music through the keys. And, a dying star whispers into my ears, "I am not an expert at brown nosing. So I rely on discipline and hard work to get me places in the world." And, I think a dying star is so ambitious. Where would a dead star go if it succeeds in life.

Elton John sits on the bench of his piano and plays a song for one dying star.

"It's music to my ears," says the star amusingly to himself.

At Chautauqua, in the nether region of the cosmos, a very

successful businessman advises me on my writing life. He is a twig, part of a branch of a tree, and he says, "Vi, monetize your imagination. Behave like you are an old white guy. And be a griffin good."

I sit down and study the weather patterns of my soul. My body. There is climate change everywhere. My hands, feet, and nose used to feel cold. Now they are like heating pads I could place over my stomach whenever I have menstrual cramps. I used to stare coldly at the closed sign at an ice cream parlor because they wouldn't sell ice cream in the winter months. They shut down for six months out of the year so they could play the flute to an almond tree. I want to be the dolphin that gets high on pufferfish. I am not Nietzsche, but I need, I just need, my neurotoxin. I am not an elephant seal—

Biting into a pufferfish will paralyze me. Probably not from the waist down. Probably from the tongue and up. Though emotionally—I am experiencing reverse climate change in my heart. I used to want to hug everyone, especially when I walked down the streets and it was verdant and the world was not gray and half-full with nasty pollutants. But, now my heart is swollen with hatred for humanity.
Could heart surgery remove hate?

I am still facing the danger. The aftermath. The side effects of TBI, not quite the same as FBI. Traumatic brain injury after chest trauma from open-heart surgery.
What is it like to be in a concussed state?
I see patches of light. I am hypersensitive to light. My brain hurts randomly at different times of the day. I wake up with

consistent ringing in my ears. And, there are 24.9 kilos of clouds weighing down in my consciousness. I can't seem to pin a balloon down with my memory.

Has anyone ever physically touched someone's heart? A lover even? Certainly never a lover. My Pakistan nurse kept on saying, "I just can't believe someone not just figuratively but literally and corporeally touched your heart." In case you didn't know: the heart is usually concealed inside the body. Usually lives inside the bone cage like a prisoner. In a maximum-security prison. To break this supermax calcified correctional facility or cardiovascular penal institution as some of you like to call it, a saw is needed. Preferably an electric one. After he used a saw, then he took a knife. The surgeon then had to make an incision into my heart so he could operate on the valve. And, the heart can't be wet. And, if it's wet, he can't operate on it. So, my blood (about 3.5 quarts of it) had to take an Uber and then rent an Airbnb from a perfusionist who was happy to rent out a heart-and-lung machine for my body. Has my heart ever lost a belt buckle to a perfusionist before?

There are pins and needles wherever once I realized that my friend lost her decade-old belt to a guy whom she fucked and met on Tinder.
But who steals a belt?

Then I recalled my film theorist friend who lives in LA, I remember her exact words, "He was so confident about the profoundness of his good intention that he thought little things, like the details of his contract, were insignificant." Then I remember, they were significant to me. Very significant. Now, because of him, my paycheck from teaching is delayed a week and then another week.

I don't want to amputate hate. I want to preserve it like how fish factories preserve sardines. Just stack them high. Just stack them.

V K N

COMPONENT	RESULT	UNITS	RANGE
White Blood Cell Count	4.4	Thousand/uL	3.8–10.8
Red Blood Cell Count	3.91	Million/uL	3.80–5.10
Hemoglobin	11.4	g/dL	11.7–15.5
Hematocrit	34.9	%	35.0–45.0
MCV	89.2	fL	80.0–100.0
MCH	29.1	pg	27.0–33.0
MC	32.7	g/dL	32.0–36.0
RDW	21.7	%	11.0–15.0
Platelet Count	203	Thousand/uL	140–400
MPV	8.6	fL	7.5–12.5
Absolute Neutrophils	2543	cells/uL	1500–7800
Absolute Lymphocytes	1527	cells/uL	850–7800
Absolute Monocytes	251	cells/uL	200–950
Absolute Eosinophils	48	cells/uL	15–500
Absolute Basophils	31	cells/uL	0– 20
Neutrophils	57.8	%	
Lymphocytes	34.7	%	
Monocytes	5.7	%	
Eosinophils	1.1	%	
Basophils	0.7	%	
Iron, Total	61	mcg/dL	40–190
Iron Binding Capacity	251	mcg/dL	250–450
% Saturation	24	% (calc)	11–50
Ferritin	38	ng/mL	10–154

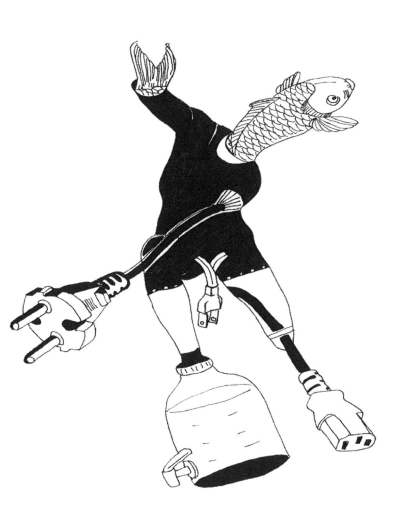

ABOUT THE AUTHOR

Vi Khi Nao's work includes poetry, fiction, film, play, and cross-genre collaboration. She is the author of the novels *Swimming With Dead Stars* (FC2, 2022) and *Fish in Exile* (Coffee House Press, 2016), the story collections *The Vegas Dilemma* (11:11 Press, 2021) and *A Brief Alphabet of Torture* (winner of the 2016 FC2 Ronald Sukenick Innovative Fiction Prize), and five poetry collections: *A Bell Curve Is A Pregnant Straight Line* (11:11 Press, 2021), *Human Tetris* (11:11 Press, 2019), *Sheep Machine* (Black Sun Lit, 2018), *Umbilical Hospital* (1913 Press, 2017), and *The Old Philosopher* (winner of the 2014 Nightboat Books Prize for Poetry). She was the Fall 2019 Shearing Fellow at the Black Mountain Institute.

www.vikhinao.com

ACKNOWLEDGMENTS

Some of the poems in this collection have appeared in the following journals, sometimes in slightly different forms:

POETRY
THE WANDERER
THE THOUGHT EROTIC
PANGYRUS
THE2RIVERVIEW
BLACKBIRD
BONE BOUQUET
GETTYSBURG REVIEW
BEST AMERICAN POETRY BLOG
HEAVY FEATHER REVIEW
ZOCALO PUBLIC SQUARE
THE FOURTH RIVER
TAOS JOURNAL OF INTERNATIONAL
POETRY & ART
VESTIGES
BRINK

BLACK SUN LIT is a print and digital literary press that endeavors to introduce, promote, and support both emerging and experienced writers whose work has little representation—or minimal exposure—in a reading world largely governed by commercial publishing.

We propose a renewed aestheticism that values beauty—not communication or identification—as the end of literature. Beauty is for us the experience of the limit, an autonomy beyond that of life itself. We search for it in all forms of extreme expression: whether in minimalism or maximalism, ultramodernism or neotraditionalism, in the experimental or in the archaic, in a desire that exceeds the body or in the longing for boredom. Beauty is the encounter between the saint and the hedonist, the prostitute and the Buddha: a truth that, like staring into the face of Medusa, petrifies the gaze into a contemplation of nothingness. At Black Sun Lit we value beauty that can be discerned in the fragmentary and the sacred, the dysfunctional and the erotic, the derelict and the obsessive.

Subscribe to the BSL mailing list to receive notifications about new print and digital releases, open reading periods, submission guidelines, events, news, and more.

@BlackSunLit
www.blacksunlit.com/subscribe

Forthcoming

———

Vestiges_06: *Aporia*
Suede Mantis / Soft Rage by Jennifer Soong
Material Exercises by Blanca Varela, trans. Carlos Lara
No Material by Losarc Raal

Available Now

———

I am writing ~~you~~ from afar by Moyna Pam Dick
Vestiges_05: *Lacunae*
Apostasy by Katy Mongeau
Vestiges_04: *Aphasia*
Naked Thoughts by Róbert Gál, trans. David Short
Sheep Machine by Vi Khi Nao
Situ by Steven Seidenberg
Vestiges_03: *Mimesis*
Gnome by Robert Lunday
Vestiges_02: *Ennui*